GROW YOUR MIND

FACE YOUR FEARS

Written by Alice Harman
Illustrated by David Broadbent

W
FRANKLIN WATTS
LONDON•SYDNEY

Franklin Watts
First published in Great Britain in 2020 by The Watts Publishing Group
Copyright © The Watts Publishing Group, 2020

Produced for Franklin Watts by
White-Thomson Publishing Ltd
www.wtpub.co.uk

Alice Harman has asserted her right to be identified as the author of this
Work in accordance with the Copyright, Designs and Patents Act 1988.

Series Designer: David Broadbent
All illustrations by: David Broadbent

Every attempt has been made to clear copyright. Should there be any
inadvertent omission please apply to the publisher for rectification.

Printed in China

Franklin Watts
An imprint of
Hachette Children's Group
Part of The Watts Publishing Group
Carmelite House
50 Victoria Embankment
London EC4Y 0DZ

An Hachette UK Company
www.hachette.co.uk
www.franklinwatts.co.uk

Facts, figures and dates were correct when going to press.

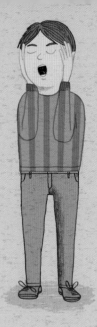

A trusted adult is a person
(over 18 years old) in a child's
life who makes them feel safe,
comfortable and supported.
It might be a parent, teacher,
family friend, care worker
or another adult.

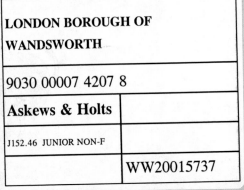

CONTENTS

Fear and mindsets

Sometimes it can seem like other people don't get scared at all, like you're the only one. But that's just not true!

Everyone has to deal with **fears and worries** sometimes – even your strictest teacher, even your loudest classmate, even your favourite celebrity.

You can't learn to never feel fear – and you shouldn't want to! Fear can sometimes help to **keep us safe** and make good choices.

But you can learn how best to face your fears so that they don't stop you from **feeling happy** and doing what you want in life.

We sometimes think of our brains as being fixed the way they are. We call this a **fixed mindset**. It can make it feel like our fears will stay with us forever, and never feel any easier to understand and manage.

But in reality, our brains are always **growing and changing**. Billions of neurons in your brain constantly pass messages to each other along connecting paths, and what you think and do can build and strengthen connections that help you face your fears.

In fact, even just believing that you have the ability to learn and change is a really great start. We call this a **growth mindset**, and this book will help you to develop it.

Let's get started!

What are you afraid of?

The first step in learning how to face our fears is working out **what they actually are**! For instance, you might be scared of reading aloud in class. Think about it – why do you have this fear?

Breaking down our fears in this way helps us to **see them more clearly**, and better understand exactly why we feel scared. Then we can start thinking about what we can do to manage our fears.

Is it that you don't like the feeling of everyone looking at you? Could that be because you're worried that you'll make a mistake in front of them – and that they'll be mean about it or think badly of you?

Ask a trusted adult to help you create **mind maps** that break down your three biggest fears. Talk through each fear in turn. What about them makes you feel afraid?

Mind map

Let's imagine you're scared of the sea. **Why?** It could be the idea of fish touching you, waves knocking you over, the ground sinking under your feet, sharks in the deep water, or something else.

What positive actions could you take to help you feel safer and more able to face this fear? Write an **action plan** with your trusted adult and check in once a week to talk over how you feel it's going.

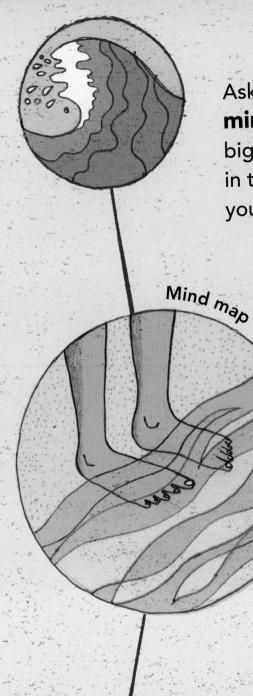
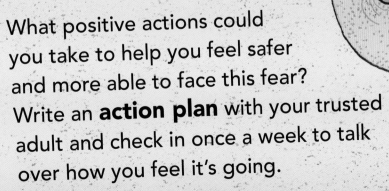

Give it a minute

When your brain thinks that it needs to protect you from danger, a kind of **'fear switch'** flips inside it. This floods your body with substances, such as adrenaline, that make you feel like running or getting angry or freezing on the spot. You might feel your heart pounding in your chest or a rush of cold through your body.

Your brain is trying to keep you safe by preparing your body to **escape or overcome the threat**, but if you're not actually in danger it's not very helpful!

If you feel this 'fear switch' flip and you start getting all panicky, just give yourself a minute to **calm down**. You'll then be able to think more clearly and find it easier to behave in a way that you choose, rather than acting out of fear.

Here are some ways that you could pass a minute and try to calm yourself down. Think of some of your own ideas, too.

You could:

★ take some deep **'umbrella breaths'**, imagining your belly opening up like an umbrella as you breathe in and slowly closing again as you breathe out

★ **count slowly** up to 20 and back down again, imagining each number having a different colour or pattern

★ sing one of your **favourite songs** in your head

★ picture all your **favourite people and things** – foods, animals, fun places, toys – anything you like.

You're not alone

Sometimes you **might not want to talk** about your fears, perhaps because you're embarrassed or because it feels too hard to say them out loud. You might also feel like you should be able to deal with your fears by yourself. But this can feel really lonely, and make the fears even worse.

Remember that your trusted adults want to help you deal with your fears, so always **let them know** if you're scared or worried about something.

Not all fears are ones that you should learn to face, either. If you're scared because someone is hurting or bullying you, or doing things that make you feel bad or strange, that's something that just needs to stop. Tell a trusted adult so they can help **keep you safe**.

Alfie

When I stayed at my grandma's house,
most of the time it was fine. But I was always
scared about accidentally making a mess, breaking
something or being too loud because **my grandma
suddenly got so angry.**

She'd shout really loudly in my face, grab my arm so hard that it really
hurt and shut me outside in the garden for ages as punishment.

I felt too nervous to tell my dads for a while, but one day I was so scared
of going that I ended up bursting into tears and **telling them everything.**

They were really glad I'd told them, and said it was for them to sort out
now and that I did the right thing by not ignoring my
scared feelings. Now I know that I can **ask them
for help,** and that it's wrong for adults
to make me feel scared.

Meet your fears

Sometimes, fears are obvious – if you think about them, you feel really **scared or nervous** right away. You might even feel shaky, get a stomach ache or feel sick.

But sometimes fears are **hidden inside other feelings**. Being scared can make us feel weak, so we may cover it up with another feeling, like anger, without even knowing we're doing it. We might also worry that our fear is silly, and so not want to admit to it.

But if something makes you feel scared, then that's all that matters. And whatever it is, there will definitely be other people who get **just as scared** as you about it!

With a trusted adult, try both listing things that:

 **you really don't like**

 **make you feel angry**

⭐ **you refuse to do and say are stupid.**

For example, maybe you think playing sports is stupid. But, actually, might it be that you're scared of not doing well, so it feels better to **pretend you don't care**?

Talk about your lists and try to work out whether some of the things you wrote down might make you feel a bit scared or worried. Then make some **mind maps** to get to know these fears better, as you did in the activity on page 7.

Being brave

Being brave doesn't mean never feeling scared – that's **impossible**! And it doesn't mean ignoring fear either.

Bravery is about working to **overcome our fears**. We all have different fears, so what might be easy for one person to do might take a huge amount of bravery for someone else.

For example, someone with no fear of heights isn't being brave when they travel in a lift all the way to the top floor of a tall building. But someone who is afraid of heights might need to be **very brave** to do that.

By facing our fears, and dealing with uncomfortable feelings, we help ourselves feel freer and less afraid in the long term. That's **real bravery**!

Selim

My parents took me to a show at the community centre down the road and it was so good! One of the groups was all kids around my age who played **traditional music** together, and my dad said I could join if I wanted.

I really wanted to, but they were so good I was scared they wouldn't want me. The first time I tried to go to a practice, my dad walked me up to the door but then I got so scared I made him take me back home again.

I felt really bad and silly, but my dad told me it was **totally natural to get scared sometimes**. We practised playing on my dad's traditional musical instruments a bit at the weekend, then the next week I went back and we walked in together.

Everyone was really friendly and they didn't mind that I was a beginner at all. The teacher showed me some basic notes and I played along right away. I felt really **proud of myself** for being brave, and I love music group now!

LITTLE STEPS

Although your brain is always growing and learning, making big changes to the way you think – for example, being able to manage your fears – takes a bit of **time and effort**.

If you're scared about something and don't want to be, this might feel **frustrating**. You might think, 'That's not fast enough, I need to stop feeling scared right now'.

But give your brain a chance! Take things **step by step**, and you'll be making progress all the time. Although at first it might feel slow and difficult, if you keep going you can help really change the way your brain thinks about your fears – hopefully for good.

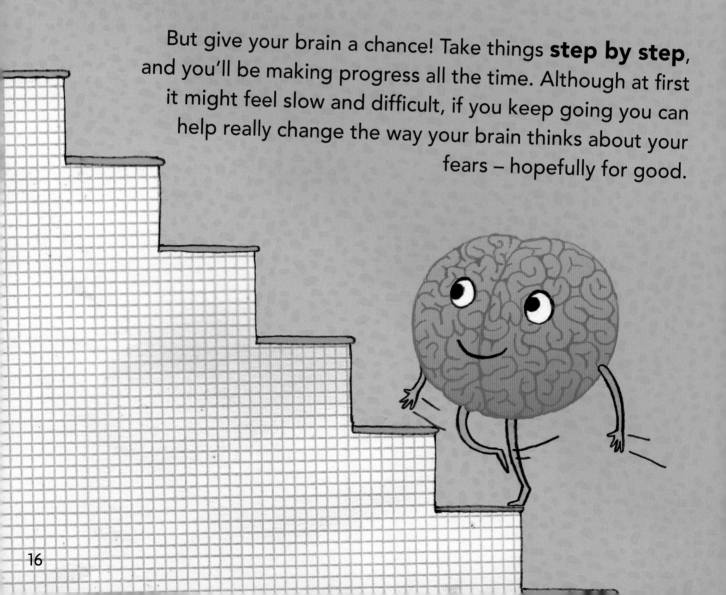

With a trusted adult, create a **step-by-step action plan** to help your brain manage your fears.

First, think about what the **ultimate goal** of facing your fear would look like. For example, if you're afraid of the dark it might be, 'I will try to go to sleep with the lights turned off'. On a piece of paper, draw a ladder with this goal at the top.

Talk with your trusted adult about what you find scary about sleeping in the dark. How could you break down your journey towards this goal into **smaller steps** that feel less scary?

Perhaps you could start by keeping your bedroom door open and the light on outside. Then you might close the door bit by bit, and eventually sleep in complete darkness. Write these actions on the steps going up the ladder, and colour them in as you **climb towards your goal**!

Big leaps

Even when we break our fear-facing journeys down into smaller steps, there are still moments when to make progress we have to really **challenge ourselves**.

These 'big leaps' forwards might make us feel quite worried or scared. We can also end up thinking of them in a **fixed-mindset way** (see page 5), as moments where we will either succeed or fail to face our fears.

For example, if we're nervous about sleeping anywhere that isn't our own home, going over to a friend's house for our first sleepover might feel like a 'big leap'. And getting too upset and needing to go home could feel like we've failed. But that's **not true at all**!

These 'big leaps' are just part of a long learning journey. It isn't important that they go perfectly, what matters is **what we learn from them** and how we move on with our journey.

Laura

When my friend Daisy invited me to her birthday sleepover party, it sounded like so much fun but I couldn't stop worrying about having to **stay the night** in a strange place.

I talked to my mum and stepdad and they were really nice. We agreed that I would go to the party, because I didn't want to miss out, but that they would come and pick me up at any time if I wanted to go home.

I had fun at the party, but as we were going to bed I felt so worried that I got a bad tummy ache and I couldn't get to sleep. I told Daisy's mum, and my parents **came to pick me up** right away.

I felt embarrassed at first, and like I'd failed, but no one minded at all. They were just happy I'd tried and I hadn't missed the party altogether. I felt much better knowing that there was **no pressure**, and at the next sleepover I went to I stayed the whole night!

NOW ISN'T THEN

When you have a bad experience,
you might be scared about it happening
again and try to **avoid** anything you
connect to that experience.

For example, if one time you bit into an apple and got
a rotten bit, it might make you feel worried about eating
an apple in future **in case it happens again**. This is your
brain's way of trying to protect you.

But with most apples you'll just get a lovely sweet crunch,
not a horrible rotten taste. It would be a shame to never
eat an apple again because of **one bad experience**!

If you know that something is safe, try
to **help your brain understand** that
having one bad experience doesn't mean
the same thing will happen every time.

Rahim

I always used to love going to the playground to spend time with my friends, until one day I fell off the **big climbing frame** and really hurt myself.

Then, when we got home, I realised I'd lost my favourite tiger that I always liked to keep in my pocket. My mum went back but she couldn't find it.

I didn't want to go back to the playground ever again, even though it meant not seeing my friends there. But my mum helped me think about **all the other nice times** I'd had there, and I realised that having one bad time didn't mean it couldn't be fun again.

I agreed to go back, but to just go on the swings to begin with – and to empty my pockets and give everything to my mum first.

STORY TIME'S OVER

Our **imagination** is an amazing thing. It helps us create stories and games and all sorts of other fun things. But sometimes it can also be really unhelpful – especially when it comes to our fears.

When we are scared or worried, we often tell ourselves **horrible stories** about what's going to happen. It can feel like just by imagining these terrible things, we're going to make them come true – like some sort of bad magic.

We might even start doing certain actions, like touching or counting things, to make us feel like we're stopping these bad things from happening.

It's important to **talk to a trusted adult** if you're having difficult feelings, so they can help you manage your worries.

Talk with a trusted adult about something that scares you and write down the **worst version** of what you're worried might happen.

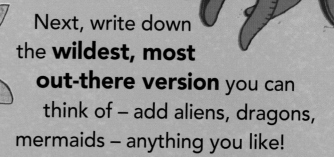

Next, write down the **wildest, most out-there version** you can think of – add aliens, dragons, mermaids – anything you like!

For example, maybe your 'worst fear' version of having a birthday party is that no one will come. Your 'wildest' version might be that it gets invaded by a pack of flying monkeys and they steal all your birthday cake!

Does imagining the strange creatures in your 'wildest' version mean they will appear? No! It's a story – and the 'worst fear' version is, too. No one can predict the future, and thinking something **doesn't make it come true**.

When you find your thoughts spiralling into negative, scary stories, try repeating **'That's a story'** in your head – or out loud. Check in with a trusted adult so they can help you, too.

See the other side

When we feel really scared about something, it can be hard to ever imagine not being scared. What would that even look like?

Well, try picturing it! One really helpful way to develop a growth mindset (see page 5) is to **visualise** yourself managing your fears.

For example, if you're scared of horses you could **imagine yourself happy** and smiling as you stroke one on the neck.

Thinking positively about facing your fears can give you a **great boost** to keep on trying – even when things feel really challenging. Give it a go!

Roisin

When I started swimming lessons at school,
I didn't know what to expect and it made me
feel **really nervous**.

I was especially afraid of going underwater, and I felt like I'd never
be able to put my head below the surface. I talked to my auntie
about it, and she showed me how to **visualise myself swimming**.

I made a picture in my mind where I was swimming along
underwater beside my auntie. We were both smiling and
having a nice time together. I **described it out loud** to my
auntie, and thought about how the water would feel, how
it would sound and so on, so it felt real.

The next time I went to the pool, I felt so much more
positive! I'm **making good progress** and feeling really
proud of myself for trying so hard.

INNER CRITIC

Sometimes the thing we're most scared of isn't anything like snakes or spiders. It's a **voice inside our head** telling us we're not good enough and we don't deserve good things to happen.

This voice can be the reason we don't want to try new challenges, and it can make us feel really bad if we don't do everything perfectly the first time.

The most important thing you can do if you're thinking these mean, untrue things about yourself is to **talk to a trusted adult**. Just by sharing your difficult thoughts and feelings, you can really help them fade away.

You can also try to develop a more helpful, positive **growth mindset** (see page 5) by thinking about your life as a journey and reminding yourself of how many things you've already learned over the years.

Jon

Last year, I was **getting into a lot of trouble** at school for messing around in class and not paying attention. The school called my parents in, but I didn't want to talk about what was really wrong.

The thing was, I wasn't trying hard in class because I didn't think I was 'clever' enough to bother. I was scared that if I made any effort, I'd find out I was right. As long as I messed around, I could just blame it on my behaviour.

My teacher talked to me about developing a **growth mindset**, and we tried some practice activities. I realised that it was unhelpful to think of anyone as 'clever' or 'not clever', and that really took the pressure off me.

Since then, I've been focusing on **putting in effort** and I feel so much better. The voice in my head is much nicer to me now!

Hard to hear

It can feel really scary to imagine people telling us that we've **done something wrong**, and it can make us act in a nervous or defensive way.

Sometimes people might be being unfair or mean, and that's not helpful. But listening to **constructive feedback** – where someone is trying to teach you something as kindly as possible – can be really helpful for growing your brain.

By facing up to our fear of hearing anything negative about the way we've acted, we can make sure not to miss these helpful **learning opportunities**.

We can also teach our brain that **everyone makes mistakes**, but what counts is how we make it up afterwards.

To start off, you and a trusted adult should each write down something that you are scared someone – a friend, family member, teacher or anyone else – might say to you.

Talking with your trusted adult, decide whether your example is just mean or whether it might be **trying to be helpful**. If you think it's trying to be helpful, what could you learn from it? And what positive steps could you take to put this learning into action?

For example, 'You're stupid' is always mean, untrue and unhelpful. On the other hand, 'You've hurt my feelings' isn't nice to hear either, but it could be a good opportunity to **learn and grow**.

What if I've hurt someone's feelings?

If you've hurt someone's feelings, you can think about what you've done and how you could **make things right**. You can try to change your behaviour in future to avoid hurting others.

KEEP FACING YOUR FEARS!

Read through these tips for a quick reminder
of how you can learn to face your fears.

Make **mind maps** to break down your fears
and work out exactly what makes you feel afraid.

If you feel panicky, **take a minute** to do something that helps calm you down.

Always **talk to a trusted adult** about your fears, even if that feels difficult.

Find **hidden fears** by thinking about things that
make you angry or that you say are stupid.

Remember that **being brave** is about working
through your fears, not ignoring them.

Create a **step-by-step plan** to help your brain learn
to manage your fears over time.

Think of facing your fears as an **ongoing journey**,
not as moments where you succeed or fail.

Remember that **one bad experience** doesn't
mean the same thing will happen every time.

When you find yourself imagining that horrible things are going to happen,
remind yourself that it's **just a story** and talk to a trusted adult.

Visualise a future version of yourself managing your fears to help
you believe it's possible.

Don't listen to the **mean voice in your head** telling you that
you're not good enough – talk to a trusted adult about it instead.

Accept that **everyone makes mistakes** and think about them
as learning opportunities.

Notes for parents and teachers

The concept of a **'growth mindset'** was developed by psychologist Carol Dweck, and is used to describe a way in which effective learners view themselves as being on a constant journey to develop their intelligence. This is supported by studies showing how our brains continue to develop through our lives, rather than intelligence and ability being static.

Responding with a growth mindset means being eager to learn more and seeing that making mistakes and getting feedback about how to improve are important parts of that journey.

A growth mindset is at one end of a continuum, and learners move between this and a 'fixed mindset' – which is based on the belief that you're either smart or you're not.

A fixed mindset is unhelpful because it can make learners feel they need to 'prove' rather than develop their intelligence. They may avoid challenges, not wanting to risk failing at anything, and this reluctance to make mistakes – and learn from them – can negatively affect the learning process.

Help children develop a growth mindset by:

- giving specific positive feedback on their learning efforts, such as 'Well done, you've been practising …' rather than non-specific praise such as 'Good effort' or comments such as 'Clever girl/boy!' that can encourage fixed-mindset thinking

- sharing times when you have had to persevere learning something new and what helped you succeed

- encouraging them to keep a learning journal, where they can explore what they learn from new challenges and experiences

- helping them understand which fears are appropriate for them to work on managing (with trusted adults' guidance and support) and which situations – such as bullying – are not something they should have to face, and need to be handled by adults.

Glossary

adrenaline
a natural substance that your body produces when it thinks you are in danger

constructive feedback
when someone is trying to teach you how to do something differently, in a kind and supportive way

defensive
feeling worried or angry about being criticised

growth mindset
thinking about your brain as something that changes and grows, rather than something fixed that makes you either clever or not clever

neurons
cells in your brain that pass information back and forth between one another

umbrella breath
a slow, deep breath in which you imagine your belly opening and closing like an umbrella

visualise
to picture something in your mind that you would like to come true in future

Index

GROW YOUR MIND

978 1 4451 6860 9
978 1 4451 6861 6

978 1 4451 6923 1
978 1 4451 6924 8

978 1 4451 6925 5
978 1 4451 6926 2

978 1 4451 6927 9
978 1 4451 6928 6

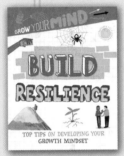

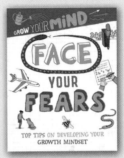

978 1 4451 6930 9
978 1 4451 6929 3

978 1 4451 6931 6
978 1 4451 6932 3

978 1 4451 6933 0
978 1 4451 6934 7

978 1 4451 6935 4
978 1 4451 6936 1

Series contents

Boost Your Brain
- A brain-boosting mindset
- Sshhhhhhh...
- One thing at a time
- Think, rest, repeat
- Brain hugs
- Time out
- Take care of your body
- Brain dump
- Picture this
- Sum it up
- Make a mnemonic
- Study buddies
- Brainy book

Make Mistakes
- Mistakes and mindsets
- Feeling down
- Think again
- Types of mistake
- A new strategy
- A-ha!
- A healthy brain
- Time to shine
- Trying new things
- Don't give up
- Challenge o'clock
- My best mistake
- Famous failures

Think Positive
- A positive mindset
- Half-full or half-empty
- All or nothing
- Celebrate
- Thanks for everything
- Smile!
- Truly positive
- Let it go
- Feelings detective
- Seeing the future
- Positive people
- Doing good
- Be kind to yourself

Don't Panic
- A calm mindset
- Future friend
- Nervous or excited?
- Trust yourself
- Not a competition
- Panic button
- Reach out
- Everything changes
- Do your research
- What can I do?
- What could go wrong?
- If it does go 'wrong'
- Tomorrow is another day

Build Resilience
- A resilient mindset
- The power of 'yet'
- Effort thermometer
- Digging deeper
- Halfway there
- Try to fail
- Positive practice
- Stronger together
- Change for good
- Seeing the future
- Ups and downs
- Rest and recover
- Get creative

Work Smarter
- Mindsets at work
- Fighting fit
- Get chunking!
- Give it your all
- Activate your brain
- Just right
- Give your brain a chance
- Keep repeating
- Nobody's perfect
- How do they do it?
- Know yourself
- Work smart, play smart
- Be the teacher!

Face Your Fears
- Fear and mindsets
- What are you afraid of?
- Meet your fears
- You're not alone
- Being brave
- Little steps
- Big leaps
- Now isn't then
- Story time's over!
- Give it a minute
- See the other side
- Energy swap
- A year from today

Ask For Help
- Help and mindsets
- Everyone needs help
- Be brave
- Speaking up
- No stupid questions
- Who can help?
- Helping others
- Team power
- Taking feedback
- Sharing opinions
- Working through challenges
- Reaching out
- Helping yourself

FRANKLIN
WATTS